An Everyday Adventure Series
by Moji Taiwo

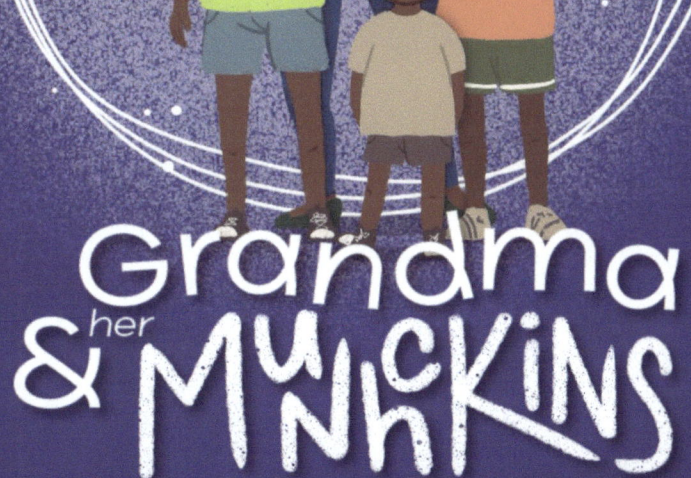

Grandma
& her Munchkins

Winter Activities with Grandma

Illustrations by Cristiana Tercero

For my precious Munchkins: Ezra, Caxton, and Amos.
Spending time with you boys brings me vitality and endless joy.

Copyright © Moji Taiwo

All rights reserved. No part of this book may be reproduced by any mechanical, photographic, or electronic process or in the form of phonographic recording; nor may it be stored in a retrieval system, transmitted, or otherwise copied for public or private use without the prior written permission of the author at mojitaiwo1@gmail.com.
ISBN (paperback): 978-1-7782838-6-4 / ISBN (Ebook): 978-1-7751235-2-1 / ISBN (IngramSpark): 978-1-7782838-2-6

Moji Taiwo
www.mojitaiwo.com

It snows in the winter where we live.

We loved playing in the snow and building a snowman.

Before going out to play, Grandma reminded us to wear our snowsuits.
We also put on our toques, gloves and winter boots.

Grandma brought out three plastic buckets, one small, one medium and one big.

She showed us how to build a snowman!

First, we put snow in the big bucket and pack it tightly to make the base.

Grandma helped us turn them upside down.

"Oops, not so fast," Grandma said.

The first snowball broke!

Then we put snow in the medium bucket
to make the body for the base.

Next, we put snow in the small bucket
to make the head of the snowman.

We carefully added more snow to round the shapes into balls,
until we were happy with them.

Finally, Grandma gave us frozen carrots and big buttons for our snowmen.

Can you guess what we did with the carrots?

And can you guess what we did with the buttons?

We each built a snowman.

One small like Baby Munchkin,

One medium

like Junior,

and the other one was big like me!

Grandma was very cold when we finished building our snowmen.

We went inside, and Grandma made hot chocolate for us.

We put marshmallows on top of it.

We hugged Grandma to keep her warm.
She told us spooky jokes from her laugh-out-loud book.

When it was too cold to play with snow outside, we played the colours and shapes matching game, and *Snakes and Ladders*.

We threw darts and added our points.

The person with the most points at the end of the game won.

Grandma was good at this game.

We piled Jenga wood blocks and watched them grow taller.

But they fell apart when I pulled one from the shaky tower.

Junior Munchkin played guitar, and Baby played the piano.

The rest of us clapped along.

As for me, I love drawing and painting for Grandma.

What games do you enjoy playing in the winter?

www.ingramcontent.com/pod-product-compliance
Lightning Source LLC
Chambersburg PA
CBHW042251100526
44587CB00002B/103